Through the
EAST WINDOW

Through the
EAST WINDOW

··

✒

Through the EAST WINDOW

Prayers and Promises for Living with Loss

Marilyn Brown Oden

UPPER ROOM BOOKS
NASHVILLE

The Upper Room Website: http://www.upperroom.org

Unless otherwise noted, scripture quotations are from
The New Revised Standard Version of the Bible, copyright © 1989 by
the Division of Christian Education of the National Council of
the Churches of Christ in the United States of America. Used by permission.

Scripture quotations designated TEV are from the Good News Bible,
the Bible in Today's English Version–Old Testament:
Copyright American Bible Society 1976;
New Testament: Copyright © American Bible Society 1966, 1971 1976.

Scripture quotations designated JB are taken from The Jerusalem Bible,
published and copyright © 1966, 1967 and 1968 by Darton, Longman,
and Todd and Doubleday, a division of Bantam Doubleday Dell Publishing Group, Inc.
Reprinted by permission of the publishers.

Cover design: Gore Studio, Inc.

Interior design: Patricia Johnson

First printing August 1998

.............Library of Congress Cataloging-in-Publication Data.............

Oden, Marilyn Brown.
Through the east window. : prayers and promises for living with loss / by Marilyn Brown Oden.
p. cm.
Includes bibliographical references.
ISBN 0-8358-0852-1
Loss (Psychology)–Religious aspects–Christianity.
2. Consolation. I. Title.
BV4905.2.O28   1998
242'.46dc21   98-16470
                                                          CIP

Printed in the United States of America

To BISHOP RUEBEN P. JOB
with deep appreciation

Acknowledgments

I want to acknowledge and express appreciation to some of the people who were especially helpful in this work directly or indirectly through their ongoing care:

John Winn, with whom I have shared the delightful challenge of leading transition seminars for clergy and their spouses in the process of moving.

Little Liam, unable to sustain life at birth, but able to give the gift of joyful anticipation, a gentle song of memory rising softly in the silence of sadness.

John Thornburg, a United Methodist pastor in Dallas and one of God's poets, who provided helpful advice and suggestions.

Phyllis Henry, who has a gift for knowing when to extend a hand on life's pilgrimage, and who has encouraged me from the very beginning of my writing ventures.

Etta Mae Mutti, who read a portion of this manuscript and offered timely reassurance.

Dale Prothro, who shared the stirring experience of seeing the Mondrian Exhibit, including Red Tree, at the Tate Gallery in London.

The dear friends in my Wednesday morning study group, who provide growth through discussion, a sense of community, fellowship, and accountability.

My husband Bill, who continues to be a source and resource as we journey together through faith and marriage.

My grown children and their spouses—whom I also claim as my own—who bring a song to my soul.

My small grandchildren, who dance in my heart.

Contents

ℒ❤

This book is not meant to be read from cover to cover, but in sections related to our specific losses. It is a writing of the *heart*, not the *head*. It is from the point of view of a participant feeling loss and experiencing grief, rather than from the perspective of rational observation and explanation of the process of grief. My hope is that it can help heal by articulating the confusing, ambivalent feelings that loss brings.

A few years ago I attended a seminar led by Edwin Friedman, author of *Generation to Generation*. He suggested that our ability to cope is related to our capacity to view a stressful situation as proportional to the inner resources we feel we can call forth. In other words, coping with loss is affected by our view of our loss in relation to our view of our inner resources. We know that when we get a physical wound, our body responds in a way that causes either infection or healing—depending on our internal resources. Similarly when we are wounded by loss, our response can begin the healing process or it can further inflame—and our inner resources affect this response.

Friedman also spoke of the effect of seeing ourselves as victims. A victim-image fosters responses like dependence and self-pity and blame. These responses are reactive, stifling our ability to draw on our inner resources. They do not bring healing. It follows that to see ourselves as made in the image of the Creator frees us to call forth our inner resources, fostering creative responses that can help heal.

Friedman recommended developing a repertoire of responses but also suggested that our capacity to draw on this repertoire is inversely proportional to our level of anxiety. The greater our anxiety, the less able we are to call forth our inner resources. Anxiety saps our awareness of these resources and drains off energy that could be used to respond in a healthy way. Loss heightens our anxiety. Yet, faith brings a trust in God's presence, which can lower that anxiety and heighten our confidence in our spiritual resources to handle loss.

During recent years the east window has become a symbol of hope and faith for me. In *Wilderness Wanderings,* I shared my habit of beginning the day with a time of solitude, sitting beside the east window before the sun rises, my senses fully aware of the aroma of tea, the warmth of the cup in my hands, dawn's song of silence. This time for scripture and prayer brings comfort, especially during difficult periods. The sunrise and the changing colors of the sky are a daily promise of God's dynamic presence.

No matter where we are in God's world or what is going on in our lives, we can look eastward at dawn in confidence that the sun will rise. Even if the clouds of loss hang so heavy over us that we cannot see the sun, our resurrection faith promises that the day will come when we, too, will see the sunrise again.

I will
awake the dawn
and see the sunrise,
the daily present
from the Eternal Presence,
rising around the globe,
lighting first the east window,
which frames our view
  of life
  and love
  and lament.

I will
awake the dawn.
I will give thanks to you,
O Lord, among the peoples;
I will sing praises to you
among the nations.
Psalm 57:8c-9

ONE
AWAKING THE DAWN

𝒵❧

During our life journey we
frequently bob along day to
day like a tiny twig on Africa's
Zambezi River, our yesterdays
rippling gently behind us.
Ahead in the distance we see
mist rising from the great
Victoria Falls and forming
white mushroom clouds that
reach from earth to sky like a

warning on the horizon. But we float on, blue sky above us, assuming our tomorrows will look like our todays.

Then one morning we awake the dawn and begin our day in the usual way. But on this day the river begins to rush forward and sweeps us along. We hear the roar of the waterfall. Louder and louder. Closer and closer. Faster and faster. Suddenly we are hurled over the edge. We tumble down the thundering cataracts, crash against the rocks, and are dashed into the deep—our yesterdays severed from our tomorrows.

Perhaps sending us over the edge is a move that leaves us vulnerable, or the empty nest, or a life dream crushed. No! A job loss. Or career change. Or forced retirement. No! A divorce from our spouse. Or of parents. Or of a grown child, wrenching away our grandchildren. No! A heart attack. Or impairing accident. Or terminal illness. No! Or relational death as a "stranger" seizes the personality of a loved one. No! Or physical death that snatches our precious friend. Or parent. Or spouse. Or child. No! No! No!

If only we could go back! This time we would know how precious are the moments. If only we could go back! This time we would taste the fullness of each day, basking in gratitude. If only we could go back! This time we would linger at the table with our sojourners and drink fully of the cup of life.

But we *cannot* go back. The terminal word has been spoken. This word silences our words while deep inside our soul screams. It is not fair! Not now! Each morning we awake to midnight, our lives for-ever changed. The unrecoverable past lies behind us and a frightening future looms ahead. Dreaded tomorrows stretch endlessly before us in this alien space where the sun cannot rise.

The Eternal Word, the Word that was in the beginning, seeks to speak to us to offer comfort and strength. Stories from the Gospel of John whisper at the back of our minds. But the roar of the water shatters our hearing, and the mist blinds our eyes to Light. We are drowning in the swirling waters.

At this moment in time I am sitting at the east window. Two sun catchers—a cross and a butterfly—hang on the upper panes of glass. An empty space separates them, for the tomb, or cocoon, between the two is missing. This writing is about that space where there is no sun catcher, when we have experienced the cross of loss and are in a limbo time of darkness–when we are longing for the past, anxious about coping in the present, and doubtful of our ability to face the future.

Loss is loss, like air is air. Losses come to all of us, and they cannot be compared. When loss occurs, its effect on us is determined not so much by the loss itself as by how we *perceive* that loss. How do we view it? How do we frame it? What does it represent? The impact of loss and our response to it are not the same from person to person—even when the loss is the same—for our perceptions differ. Likewise our inner resources differ, not only from person to person but also from time to time within our own life.

There is a story about snowflakes in a winter storm. They fell one at a time on a branch of a massive tree. Each snowflake was so tiny and weightless that it made no impact. Soon thousands of them were thick on the limb of the tree. Then another wee snowflake fell—and the branch broke. Like those snowflakes, a series of relatively small changes can occur in our lives in a brief span of time . . . and then one more comes— and suddenly we feel the break of our ability to cope. Ongoing spiritual formation helps build up our inner strength so that we have the internal reserves needed when the challenges come.

Our spiritual dimension cannot protect us from pain, for pain is part of drinking fully of the cup of life. Neither can it hoist us back up the waterfall to bygone days. But it does not leave us powerless. Though the east-window experience of the promise of God's presence does not alter our losses, it can alter how we view them, especially when we trust that the presence of God will strengthen us to handle them.

This does not mean denying hurt. When we endure painful loss, a part of us dies and we go into the "tomb" for three days or three months or three years or three decades. But our faith is a resurrection faith, and ultimately the stone is rolled away. To some degree grief still lingers, as does the scar from the wound. We do not get *beyond* loss—we learn to live *with* it.

Seeing our loss through the frame of faith gives us confidence that at some point smooth waters lie before us as well as behind us, and a spark of hope glows in the gray ashes of our soul, hope that our hearts will heal. As Christians, trusting the Loving Holy One and affirming our resurrection faith, we look through the "east window," waiting for the sun to rise again.

*Save me, O God,
    the waters from
    my tears
rise up to my neck.
The sun catchers
    are swept away,
those reflections of the Light
that elate my soul.
I seek a foothold,
weary of weeping.*

*Save me, O God,
    for the waters
have come up to
    my neck.
I sink in deep mire,
where there is no foothold;
I have come into deep
    waters,
and the flood sweeps
    over me.
I am weary with
    my crying.*
Psalm 69:1-3

TWO
LOSING THE SUN CATCHERS

Sun catchers do just that—they catch the sun. We hang them on a window, and they filter the sunlight through their brilliant colors. At a deeper level, we accumulate symbolic sun catchers that give our lives a sense of purpose—purpose connected to place, to nurturing family relationships, to our vision and dreams for the future. Sun catchers have different shapes, sources, and symbolic meanings for each of us. But to all of us they are significant. They are in the foreground as we look out the window, affecting our view of life. When we move away, or face the empty nest, or find a dream shattered, it is like losing a sun catcher. We look out the window and our focus falls on the empty place where it once hung. We sense a loss of sacred purpose and we experience the grief process.

We go through denial, searching frantically for that missing sun catcher, over and over again in the same old places. We bargain for its return, making false promises that are unrealistic and unattainable or offering to exchange a less valued sun catcher for the one lost. We grow angry at the intrusion of change, the unfairness, the deprivation. We feel a deep void both in our outer world and our inner one, a void filled by despair. Alone in a vacuum, we sometimes wonder if even God is absent.

During a difficult time of transition after losing a sun catcher, I had one of the most vivid dreams of my life:

The guard leads me into a barren prison cell and closes the door behind me. Steel clangs against steel and echoes down the row of cells.

I stand alone behind the bars, with no window for the sun. I have done nothing wrong. There has been no accusation. No trial. I think about how unfair this is. Yet, I do not feel angry but passive. Strangely, I am not afraid.

The guard stands beyond the bars, a matronly figure in uniform, her short brown hair matching her expressionless eyes. She looks at me without empathy nor judgment, simply doing the duty required by her job, detached from it all.

As the guard turns to leave, I ask, "Am I able to have paper and pencil?"

She nods that I can.

"And books to read?"

Again a nod. She does not bother to speak.

Those two nods enfold me in a sense of calm and peace. I can still write! I can still read! I will be all right!

When I awoke, I felt blessed with a message of comfort and encouragement. The power of that dream stayed with me throughout the throes of that transition and is still with me even today.

Loss casts us on the wrong side of the bars separating the way things were from the way we want them to be. It comes without our invitation (though perhaps with our permission). It is not the result of our wrongdoing. There is no accusation against us and no trial in which to plead our case before a judge or a jury of our peers. But our freedom to live as we did in the past is taken away. It feels unfair, undeserved. And it goes unnoticed. Others appear indifferent to our loss, going about their business as usual.

A twofold question rises from deep within our soul: "Will I still have a sacred purpose? Will I still have the sources I need to help me fulfill it?"

"Yes!" comes the cosmic answer. Probably not without change. Perhaps not as easily, not as clearly. But we are continually offered a sacred purpose for our life. And no one has to seek this fulfillment alone. The Spirit is always present. Bars cannot keep out spiritual growth; they may even deepen it. The only danger is within us, by ignoring or neglecting that growth.

During the early part of this decade, I participated in a prison ministry in Ekatkerinburg, Russia. The new Christians inside that prison had received permission to decorate the wall where they held worship services. On that bare wall they painted a window and a rainbow, the rainbow appearing to begin outside in the free world sky and arching inside the "window" and down the prison wall. *They would be all right!*

This awareness does not change the situation, but in time it can change our feelings about the situation. It can free us from paralysis. We can plug the energy formerly drained by anxiety and funnel that energy into a creative response. We can look toward the horizon and watch assumed boundaries recede. When we stand behind a barred door slammed shut by a move, by the empty nest, or by the loss of a dream, we can be assured that the loving gaze of God is upon us. In faith and trust we paint in our mind's eye an east window, framing our view with hope. Despite the loss of a sun catcher, *we will be all right!*

When a Move Comes

Moving is a common transition, but that does not make it any less traumatic. Even when a move is a "gain," it can still be a source of pain. I have lived in six places since my husband Bill graduated from seminary. I moped through each move—then, in time, fully enjoyed the new place as much as the old.

The move following my husband Bill's consecration as a bishop was particularly difficult for me. It severed me from the sense of purpose and personal identity I experienced in my job, from my beloved community of faith, from a quarter-of-a-century support group of clergy and spouses, and it distanced our children by a thousand miles. It was during this troublesome transition that the prison dream, mentioned earlier, came to me.

Parker Palmer, in *The Active Life*, speaks of people who "have no self-sustaining identity":

> They equate selfhood with particular activities, and their vitality depends on being in places where they can

play those roles. Put them in places where their competencies are not required, and they find themselves on the thin edge of nonbeing.

I saw myself, for I had been transplanted into a situation in which my accustomed activities and competencies were neither required nor useful, and I stood "on the thin edge of nonbeing." His words helped me realize that the source of my difficulty was not caused by my *loss of identity* in this new situation, as I had thought, but by my *lack of self-sustaining identity* in the first place. It was a disconcerting insight but a starting place for growth.

Recently, after eight wonderful years in Louisiana, Bill was assigned to the Dallas Area, and once again I felt the pain of loss. Even when our identity is self-sustaining, and even when we know we will fully enjoy the next place, and even when we are excited about a new venture, moving brings us a sense of loss for it forces us to leave people we love. Catapulted into the grief process, we weave across a swaying bridge from the known to the unknown.

THE PAPER CRACKLES

The paper crackles
as I wrap the dishes, O Lord,
    dishes wet with my tears.
My feet stumble
    over empty boxes and
    full ones piled high,
taped and labeled
    with my name—
yet, I try to tell myself
I am just packing for another.

My friend calls from
    New Orleans.
She is only an hour away today
but ten, come tomorrow.
"Pretend I am standing there
on the street corner," she says,
"waving my hanky
    as you pull away."
Her voice shakes.
Our sobs duet.

I leave behind good friends
    like her, O Lord,

He [Jesus] left Judea and started back to Galilee. But he had to go through Samaria. So he came to a Samaritan city called Sychar, near the plot of ground that Jacob had given to his son Joseph. Jacob's well was there, and Jesus, tired out by his journey, was sitting by the well. It was about noon.

A Samaritan woman came to draw water, and Jesus said to her, "Give me a drink." (His disciples had gone to the city to buy food.) The Samaritan woman said to him, "How is it that you, a Jew, ask a drink of me, a woman of Samaria?" (Jews do not

*share things in common
with Samaritans.) Jesus
answered her, "If you
knew the gift of God, and
who it is that is saying to
you, 'Give me a drink,'
you would have asked
him, and he would have
given you living water."*

John 4:3-10

those who smiled with me
in the joyful times
and prayed for me
in the difficult ones.

I leave behind a culture
where hospitality is
as important as grits,
and people from
all walks of life
teach their children
that "yes" and "no"
are two-syllable words:
"Yes, ma'am," and, "No, sir."

I leave behind
meandering rivers
topped by bridges
drawn for ships
and banked by old folk
and young
fishing in the sun.
And slow-moving bayous
dotted with cypress trees
draped in Spanish moss,
silhouettes of the Mystery on
moon-slivered nights.

I leave behind the pine tree rising steadfast
beside the east window upstairs,
its stately trunk dividing
then joining again,
like palms pressed together in prayer.

For the last time, O Lord,
I trudge up those stairs
and gaze through the east window,
where countless mornings
I watched the sunrise.

I stand alone
trying to peer into the unknown,
savoring my final moments in this space
wondering if there will be an east window
in the new place.

My numbed mind recalls John's story
of the woman at the well.
I want to take your role, O Lord,
sitting by the well, tired out
by the journey to a foreign land.
I, too, feel weary and want to rest,
dreading the differences ahead
and the sojourn with strangers,

those new folk with whom I have no bond
for we share no history together.

But I know, O Lord, that in truth
I stand in the sandals of the Samaritan.
For I do not see the gift of God before me.

With a sigh I take the sun catchers down
and wrap them well to rehang another day.
Before turning away
I bow to the stately pine tree,
transformed through the years
into my prayer tree.

For the last time I bid it farewell.
O Lord, how can I fare well without it?

Facing a New East Window

Facing a new east window,
the move behind me now,
I wait for the sun.
But it does not rise.
O Lord, is the living water
made up partly of tears?

In the darkness I make out trees
across the street.
Barren of leaves,
they cluster against the cold.
Their naked limbs
form a stark silhouette,
gray upon gray.
Unlike my distant pine tree,
they do not know
     how to pray.

Perhaps I have forgotten, too.
For my prayers lack gratitude.
Mourning my loss of place
has replaced my morning
     praise.

The woman said to him [Jesus], "Sir, you have no bucket, and the well is deep. Where do you get that living water? Are you greater than our ancestor Jacob, who gave us the well, and with his sons and his flocks drank from it?" Jesus said to her, "Everyone who drinks of this water will be thirsty again, but those who drink of the water that I will give them will never be thirsty. The water that I will give will become in them a spring of water gushing up to eternal life." The woman said to him, "Sir, give me this water, so that I may never be thirsty or have to keep coming here to draw water." . . .

*The woman said to him,
"Sir, I see that you are a
prophet. Our ancestors
worshiped on this moun-
tain, but you say that the
place where people must
worship is in Jerusalem."
Jesus said to her,
"Woman, believe me, the
hour is coming when you
will worship the Father
neither on this mountain
nor in Jerusalem. You
worship what you do not
know; we worship what
we know, for salvation is
from the Jews. But the
hour is coming, and is
now here, when the true
worshipers will worship
the Father in spirit and
truth, for the Father
seeks such as these
to worship him."*
John 4:11-15, 19-23

O Lord, you told
   the woman at the well
about the living water—
water that knows no limits,
   no dams, no foreign lands.
You spoke to her of a spring
   gushing up within.
She did not understand,
wishing only to be spared
her daily trudge to the well.

How like her I am, O Lord!
Wanting magic waters
   that will spare me
daily drudge and discipline,
that will carry me quickly
once and for all
through the trauma
   of transition.

You told her that
   to truly worship
is to worship any place,
   O Lord.
I *know* that in my head,
but I do not *feel* it
   in my heart—

like words piped in on stereo
rather than sung from my soul.

I long to return to the mountain,
to the faces I recognize and love,
to the family of faith I called mine.
In this new congregation
my steps ring hollow
as I move down the aisle.
Their eyes watch me distantly,
their lips silent while I pass by.
I am a guest, a new arrival,
not a member of the family.

This seems like their house,
O Lord, not yours.
You see me smile with empty spirit,
kneel at the altar with empty soul,
accept the bread and wine with empty heart.

How I thirst for the living water!
But I cannot draw water from the well,
for it is too deep and the cord of my faith
    too frayed.
And no spring gushes up within me.
My body wraps around dry bones
    in a spiritual desert.

G od is spirit, and those who worship him must worship in spirit and truth." The woman said to him, "I know that Messiah is coming" (who is called Christ). "When he comes, he will proclaim all things to us." Jesus said to her, "I am he, the one who is speaking to you."

John 4:24-26

FROM DEEP WITHIN

From deep within, O Lord,
I feel a tug of the Spirit,
a whispering that you are here
in this new space
just as you were there
in the old place.

I hear you speak to me, O Lord,
through the scripture
about the woman at the well.
Through the ancient words
of the desert mothers
    and fathers
in the books placed once
    again on my shelf.
Through the invisible presence
of all the saints who uphold me.
And through the cluster of trees
beginning to bud,
teaching me anew how to pray.

I hear you speak to me, O Lord,
through the smile
    of my new pastor.

Through the warm greetings
    of acquaintances
who are becoming friends.
Through the familiar hymns and creeds.
And through the ancient symbols of the church
    Word
    Water
    Light
    Eucharist
calling to me from the altar,
timeless and universal.

I hear you speak to me, O Lord.
Through the sun catchers I found today
in a box mismarked and shoved aside.
Through the ones
    I reverently hang in the window
and those no longer relevant
    due to the move,
which I tenderly piece
into a stained-glass mosaic
consecrated for memories.
And through the colorful fragments
found in these rushing new waters,
fragments I carefully drop into a kaleidoscope
and swirl with my fingers,

watching the changing patterns
form possibilities for the future.

O Lord, I want to worship you
in spirit and truth.
I press my nose against the east window,
seeking my true home in you,
trusting that if I center myself in your love,
I can never be homeless again.

Following my youngest son's departure
for college, a poignant *Family Circus* cartoon appeared in the Sunday paper. Bil
Keane began with a tiny newborn and
bumped together sketches of a growing
child as the parents watched their son whisk
from infancy toward college age and beyond,
reminding us how fast the years pass and
that each day is special. Yellowed now, that
cartoon is still with me. Surely the clock and
calendar trick us in making those eighteen
years that go by so slowly for a growing
child the very same span of time that goes
by so quickly for us as parents!

Bill and I reared four children. Though
we did not view them as extensions of our
identities, they were the major focus of our
care and concern. For a quarter of a century
children enriched the lively conversation
around our table. When Bill and I sat down
together for dinner *alone* the evening after
our youngest left, I felt a scary moment of
wondering if there would be anything to talk
about!

A few parents are in family businesses or other situations in which the children either never leave home or are in revolving-door situations of leaving and returning. But for most of us that *day of departure* comes, and we know things will never be quite the same again.

Ambivalence grips us. We want our children to be independent, but we miss them. We know that they will always be in our vision, at least in the periphery, but it is unlikely that their vision will include us. We want them to have full lives without us, but we are a bit frightened of life without them. And perhaps at times we look back to their childhood days and wonder if we paid so much attention to the day-to-day triptych that we missed the journey.

However young or old we are at the time of the last child's departure, we face a passage into a different phase. It is like standing at the top of the Continental Divide and realizing the waters of our life no longer run the same way.

HE LEFT THIS MORNING

He left this morning, O Lord,
the last of my children.
He pulled out of the driveway,
all smiles. Beginning
the prologue to his manhood.

I waved and turned
    quickly away,
hiding my tears. Beginning
the epilogue of my adulthood.

It is the little things, O Lord,
that are so hard this day:

Like standing
    at the check-out stand,
placing my groceries
    on the belt—
minus nacho cheese Doritos,
Pecan Sandies,
Snickers.
The tears come again.

Like returning home and

On the third day there was a wedding in Cana of Galilee, and the mother of Jesus was there. Jesus and his disciples had also been invited to the wedding. When the wine gave out, the mother of Jesus said to him, "They have no wine."

John 2:1-3

missing his car,
missing him,
missing the way life was.

Like lying awake
with no one to listen for,
no one to wait up for,
no children left to nurture.
Empty of that which nurtured me.

Memory of daily hugs
replaces daily hugs;
it is a cold exchange.
The wine has given out, Lord,
like at the wedding in Cana;
life fades of its rich color.
There is no reason to awake the dawn.

I go outside into the moonless night
and hoe the ground
preparing a garden to tend,
hoeing deeper and deeper
quicker and quicker
bending in rhythm to my sobs.
Watering the ground with my tears.

It Seems a Small Request

It seems a small request, Lord,
like that of Mary
    at the wedding:
Please carry my love
on the wings of the wind
across the miles
to my grown children.

I used to put Band-Aids
    on scraped knees
and heal their hurts
    with a kiss,
but their stumbles
    in adulthood
are not so easily mended,
and I must blow kisses
    from a distance.
Please, Lord, raise up
    someone in my stead.

Mary told the servants
to do what you said, Lord.
When my children
    were gathered round,

*Jesus said to her,
"Woman, what
concern is that to
you and to me? My hour
has not yet come." His
mother said to the ser-
vants, "Do whatever he
tells you." Now standing
there were six stone water
jars for the Jewish rites of
purification, each holding
twenty or thirty gallons.
Jesus said to them, "Fill
the jars with water." And
they filled them up to the
brim.*
John 2:4-7

I tried to do what you taught
and to set a good example.
But in my harried fragmentation,
I was like an empty jar,
serving you on my outer journey
while neglecting my inner one.

Now, parched and thirsty
standing on crackled ground
unable to do my part
unable to fill my empty jar to the brim
unable to bring you water
to turn into wine for them,
I still ask you, O Lord, for a miracle.

Please fill my children with your spirit;
wrap your protective arms around them
and help them know the kiss of grace
and the healing balm of faith.

COULD IT BE?

Could it be, O Lord,
that good wine is still to come
even after the empty nest?
That the best wine
was not served first?

Could it be, O Lord,
that you can take
the spiritual trickle
of my busy fragmented years
and transform it into a spring
that blesses
    those around me now?

Is that the big surprise?
That our relationships
    grow deeper
as we and our children
    grow older?
That color becomes richer
    rather than fading?
That new seeds are still
    planted along the way
and burst forth in full bloom?

He [Jesus] said to them, "Now draw some out, and take it to the chief steward." So they took it. When the steward tasted the water that had become wine, and did not know where it came from (though the servants who had drawn the water knew), the steward called the bridegroom and said to him, "Everyone serves the good wine first, and then the inferior wine after the guests have become drunk. But you have kept the good wine until now."

John 2:8-10

Could it be, O Lord,
that when we hoe at midnight
a garden blossoms at sunrise?

Failed dreams are as common as chicken pox. Even when a dream is fulfilled, we tend to replace it with a new one. Or add a new dimension to it. Or immediately, like grasping the gold at the Olympics, we begin to worry about whether we will ever achieve that dream again.

Sometimes our dream lies dormant. We may be afraid to risk failure. Or our circumstances—perhaps family responsibilities—limit our freedom to spend the time necessary to achieve our dream, and we set it aside until the next stage of life . . . or permanently.

Even if we are among those rare people who seem to fulfill their dreams fairly easily, we still face a day when that will not be so. We will retire or grow ill or too old.

There are more worthy dreams than of writing books, dreams with consequences that affect the lives of people. But book dreams are the ones I know firsthand. As long as I can remember—from the time I was a child—I dreamed of being a writer.

When my first book was published while I was in my twenties, I was exceedingly joyful—but also struck by the reality that a dream can be fulfilled and the aftermath of glory remain a fantasy. My dream came true. My book came out. And nothing changed! It did not bring riches or fame or prestige.

About that same time I read *The Source* by James Michener, which became the source of my new dream—to write a novel. I did research, named the heroine "Vini," and birthed a plot—beginning with a mining story and a hero named Jamie McGregor, who died. A decade later Michener's *Centennial* was published, and I was still plodding along with family, church, and job, while my dream gathered dust on a closet shelf. Finally I completed the novel as my thesis for a master's degree in creative writing. And Sidney Sheldon's *Master of the Game* came out—beginning with a mining story and a hero named Jamie McGregor who died. My dream of a novel, now completed but unpublished, once again sits on the shelf gathering dust.

By now, I have written several nonfiction books, and I continue to see this as my "ministry." But there is a part of me that still dreams of writing fiction. And every once in a while Vini calls to me in the night.

The pain of loss when a dream is denied is shared at some point by nearly everyone—everyone who has ever dared to dream.

It was almost time for the Passover Festival, so Jesus went to Jerusalem. There in the Temple he found men selling cattle, sheep, and pigeons, and also the moneychangers sitting at their tables. So he made a whip from cords and drove all the animals out of the Temple, both the sheep and the cattle; he overturned the tables of the moneychangers and scattered their coins.

John 2:13-15 (TEV)

IT CAME WITHOUT WARNING

It came without
    warning, O God—
not with the hiss of a snake
nor a bugle charge.
The loss of my dream
came to me in silence,
waltzing in,
wearing sneakers.

My dream was
    born in my heart,
as bright as a daisy
and smelling of clover.
I nurtured it in the
    temple of my mind,
sure that it was your
    gift to me, O God,
and that its
    eventual fulfillment
would be my gift to you,
a song of praise and gratitude.
But now it lies strewed about
like old dank hay.

I thought we sat at the table together
when that dream was born, O God.
I remember facing toward you,
undergirded with bold confidence
that the journey toward my dream
was also a journey toward you.

But the table has been overturned,
the dream driven out,
the fancied coins of profit
dumped on the floor.

Lashes sting my soul
as I scan the scattered pieces
of my broken dream, my broken heart.
Hear my prayer, O God,
the Giver and Taker of dreams.

He [Jesus] told those who were selling the doves, "Take these things out of here! Stop making my Father's house a marketplace!"...The Jews then said to him, "What sign can you show us for doing this?"

John 2:16, 18

THE LOST DREAM LINGERS IN HOPELESS HOPE

The lost dream lingers
in hopeless hope,
a painful secret I keep
within the deepest part of me,
which clings still, O God,
to that mirage.

I tell myself it is not really lost.
I beg, cajole, whimper
      to make that so.
When we sat at the table
      long ago,
I opened my palms
to receive your gift.
Now I close my empty fists!
Cheated. Angry.
I claimed that dream!
Claimed it, God!
      Don't you understand!

My anger subsides,
and with a deep sigh
I ask for a sign.

My heart whispers in response,
calling me to unwelcome truth:
In the beginning, O God,
you were the Source of my dream;
you were its Center.
Then along the way my focus changed,
and I faced away from you.
I played to the marketplace,
desecrating the dream.
It was not aborted, but *mis*carried.
My vanity tainted the temple.

Now the weight of void
    stoops my shoulders,
    *dis*illusioned,
    *dis*appointed,
    *dis*regarded,
    incomplete,
    unwhole,
    unholy.
My self-portrait hangs in an empty frame.

*J*esus answered
them, "Destroy this
temple, and in three
days I will raise it up."
The Jews then said, "This
temple has been under
construction for forty-six
years, and will you raise
it up in three days?"

John 2:19-20

UNDER CONSTRUCTION
FOR MANY YEARS

Under construction
    for many years,
that dream built layer by layer
cannot be raised up again,
    O Lord,
not in three days—
nor three decades.
It is dust, blowing in the wind.

Yet, my inner storm
    is silenced.
The lightning bolts of arrogance

and the thunder booms
    of anger
have abated over time.

In the stillness after the storm
I see, O Lord, that even
    without the dream
my soul can be whole.
For a dream's ending
forces another beginning,
dislodging the old

and making way for the new—
    new perceptions
    new potentialities
    new pathways on the pilgrimage.

The Spirit breathes life
into the dust of debris,
and through faith
reshapes it once again.
What has been destroyed
can be transformed
into a new temple, untainted.

A rainbow appears,
painting a promise
that arches across the sky,
and I know that not yet,
but one day,
I will move beyond pain
and remember the joy
of dreaming that dream—
that beautiful sun catcher.
And I will smile at the memory
and give thanks, O Lord,
for it is better to have a dream
and lose it
than never to dream at all.

O that I had wings! I
would flee far away
from this sunless space,
where I look for the moon,
seeking a reflection of light
in the absence of light.
I stand at the edge of the abyss
between what was and
    what will be.
Afraid to leap in the dark,
I feel myself shoved,
free-falling through space
as in a childhood dream,
longing to be caught
    on a cloud and
cradled tenderly
    in the arms of God,
till I can soar once more.

O that I had
wings like a dove!
I would fly away and be
at rest; truly, I would flee
far away; . . .
But I will trust in you.
Psalm 55:6-7, 23

THREE
LOOKING FOR THE MOON

Sometimes the changes
that intrude into our lives are
so wrenching that we not only
lose the sun catchers, we also

lose the sun. Divorce, termination of job, or sudden impairment of physical capabilities jettison us into the frozen midnight of a Siberian winter. Giving up on the sun, we look for the moon.

It is not always easy to find the moon. Not only does it have no light of its own, but it also has a shadow side and hides among the clouds besides. Because its surface is made up of dark gray rocks and dust, it reflects only one-tenth of the light it receives from the sun. The moon constantly changes speed and distance from us and is pulled two directions at once—both toward the earth by gravity and away from the earth by centrifugal force. The one thing we can count on is its rhythm—new moon to full, waxing and waning.

Like the moon we, too, have a shadow side that can get the best of us when we are vulnerable. We, too, reflect the light of the Son, but the dust of despair and the stones of doubt block our ability to reflect that light fully. We, too, shrink and grow and shrink again, and our spiritual journey slows and speeds and slows again. We distance our-

selves from God and then, often motivated
by desperation, we practice the spiritual dis-
ciplines and begin to close the gap again.
We, too, are pulled in two directions at once.
We are weighted down by dwelling on the
past, which may have been painful but
offered the security of the known. And
simultaneously, we spin toward a future out
of control, one we do not even know how to
envision.

Our loss confuses us. We gaze out the
window but the darkness mirrors our own
reflection, dim and surreal. Our image
appears distorted without that accustomed
job or partner or physical agility that was so
much a part of our identity. We know who
we were and the future we had anticipated,
but we are confused about who we are now
without that missing chunk of our old per-
sonhood.

Even when a divorce is "friendly," it is pre-
ceded by pain and followed to some degree
by disorientation. Even when a career
comes to an end with a timely and celebrat-
ed retirement, it still forces us to contend
with the lost portion of identity linked to

work. Healing is more difficult and our woundedness deepens when we view ourselves as victims of betrayal. Betrayal by spouse in a divorce. Betrayal by employer when termination is forced. Betrayal by the body when impairment is faced. We are apt to be obsessed by the past—stone-blind to new possibilities.

One passage in *The Way of Chuang Tzu*, translated and edited by Thomas Merton, says:

> Life is followed by death; death is followed by life. The possible becomes impossible; the impossible becomes possible. Right turns into wrong and wrong into right–the flow of life alters circumstances and thus things themselves are altered in their turn.

Loss ends life as we have known it; yet, eventually, new life can follow loss. What was possible before—through our former work or former marriage or formerly trustworthy body—is now impossible; yet new things are now possible because we are freed from old claims and assumptions and we discover deeper reserves than we thought we had. Some of our perspectives about what seemed right or wrong before are shaded with new experiences and begin to fade, for our changed circumstances bring a different point of view, which changes our perceptions. This is not a chameleon effect—simply changing colors—but a zoom lens effect, for we see up close realities unnoticed before. Altered situations alter our responses, and our responses further alter situations. Nothing is final; nothing is without ripples.

WHEN A CAREER ENDS

One of Georgia O'Keeffe's paintings is called *The Road beyond the View.* We see a road winding its way up to a point, but we cannot see where it leads. As long as our career lasts, it is like traveling on a familiar road; but when that career stops it ends the known way and forces us to travel on the road beyond the view, unsure where it will take us.

Corporate downsizing and early retirement packages have turned job loss and career change into an epidemic. It is so common that if we have not faced it ourselves, it is likely that someone we know well has experienced it—a member of our immediate or extended family or a good friend. Knowing this dis–ease runs rampant does not lessen the individual pain. Forced career loss can be devastating, not only because it changes our lives in a major and unexpected way, but also because it feels like betrayal.

A career change, of course, is not always forced. Sometimes it is made intentionally and joyfully. Sometimes by default. For whatever reason a career ends, its loss can nip at us in unforeseen ways, for we give a large part of our waking hours to it, and it is usually a major focus in our lives.

Ultimately, a career ends by retirement— chosen or forced. From a distance retirement looks like a good stage in life. But up close, our perspective may change. While browsing in the New Orleans Historical Collection one day, I saw a small polemoscope which was a replica of those taken to the opera in yesteryear. Users could appear to be viewing the stage while the instrument was actually giving them a side glance of the people in the audience. Early on, we tend to view retirement through a polemoscope— seemingly looking directly at it but actually focusing on the side-benefits. No demands. No schedule. Just doing what we want all day long. But, as we draw close and see retirement straight on with the naked eye, our changed view gives rise to questions: *How will it feel to be so unneeded that there are no demands on me? What else do I really want to do? How will I fill all that time?*

My own career loss in counseling came by choice in a way. I moved with my husband and decided not to pick it back up again. But I still felt the pain of loss (at times still do). In the most despairing moments, I wondered how I justified my space on the planet. Then one day in my desperation, I began reading Evagrius; I heard his wisdom whisper to me from the fourth century. He rooted grief in the sacrifice of the past life for the present life. My past life, with all its familiar props and masks, had been sacrificed. And I mourned the loss. But I did not have to climb on the burning bier, for the adventure of life itself is always offered in the present! Evagrius taught me to leave behind my past cocoon and hover among the flowers of present opportunities.

Whether our career loss is forced, due to retirement, or a choice, it is not uncommon to find ourselves in the throes of grief. We may continue to smile on the outside while feeling on the inside that a major part of our identity has been amputated.

THE GREEN LIGHT HAS TURNED RED

The green light has turned red,
O Lord. My career is over.
Finished.
Wound up.
Closed.
I have been put on the
    butcher block and
    offered as a sacrifice.

I did not plan for it to
    end this soon,
predict it, prepare for it.
I was blind, O Lord,
    like the man you saw,
blind since the birth
    of my career.
I worked hard,
    giving the organization
the best part of each day
during the best days of my life.
But now my day has passed,
    they say;
night has come and
    I cannot work.

*As he
[Jesus]
walked along, he saw a
man blind from birth.
His disciples asked him,
    "Rabbi, who sinned,
this man or his parents,
that he was born blind?"
Jesus answered,
    "Neither this man nor
his parents sinned; he
was born blind so that
God's works might be
revealed in him. We
must work the works of
him who sent me while it
is day; night is coming
when no one can work."*
John 9:1-4

It is not just! They needed me once.
Told me how important I was.
Then, I had a green light—
    the right person
    in the right place
    at the right time.
Now they have switched to red, O Lord—
not yellow but red—
saying they must consider
the good of the whole,
that many jobs depend
on the organization's success.
They consumed me,
chewed me up,
and spat me out.

O Lord, I know sin
    did not cause my blindness,
but my blindness resulted in the sin
    of omission.
For during all those years,
carrying on your work did not matter to me.
It was the organization that I obeyed,
aimed to please,
whose work I did.

I donned its head phones,
filled my ears with its tapes,
lived its gospel,
shut out the whispers of my heart.

I stumbled over unseen opportunities—
forgetting to savor wondrous moments,
overlooking daily celebrations,
squandering whole seasons.
Blind to surprise, I missed the party.

O Lord, now I am left with confusion,
lack of purpose,
terror that my future
will be an endless fall
through the black hole of nothingness.
My life veers out of control
like driving on ice.

Yet, if once again
they turned on the green light,
I know, O Lord,
that I would race back,
like an addict
to a source!

As long as I am in the world, I am the light in the world." When he [Jesus] had said this, he spat on the ground and made mud with the saliva and spread the mud on the man's eyes, saying to him, "Go, wash in the pool of Siloam" (which means Sent). Then he went and washed and came back able to see. The neighbors and those who had seen him before as a beggar began to ask, "Is this not the man who used to sit and beg?". . . He kept saying, "I am the man." But they kept asking him, "Then how were your eyes opened?"

What Do You Do?

"What do you do?"
It is the first question asked,
O Lord, after an introduction.
I had not noticed that before.
Now, the question stabs me
for I have no answer.

"What do you do?"
Is the point of the question
to start a conversation?
Make a connection?
Take a shortcut
     to classification?
Is the asker's arm
poised in the air
brush in hand,
colors ready,
waiting to fill in
the paint-by-number portrait
projected by the answer?

"What do you do?"
Identity is at stake
for the question is not really
     about *do*—but *who*.

And the expected answer is,
"I am a . . . "
Not a verb, but a noun.
Now, how do I reply?
"I am a *nothing*"?

*"Are you not the one who
used to . . . ?"*
The "used to" hurts, O Lord.
When I lost my career,
did I also lose *me*?
Is who I am just who I was?
I have become a stranger
even to myself.

I wash my eyes, O Lord,
like the man you healed,
and I begin to see too clearly:
I pretended my career
    was the source
of the sun in my life,
blind to the long shadow
it cast over my journey.
It became a sun block,
    a Son block.

He answered,
    "The man called Jesus
made mud, spread it on
my eyes, and said to me,
'Go to Siloam and wash.'
Then I went and washed
and received my sight."
They said to him,
    "Where is he?"
He said,
    "I do not know."
John 9:5-12

I spent too much
    of my life in shadows—
spent it on increasing my standard of living.
And in the spending, I lost it.
Now cleansed in the pool of Siloam,
I yearn to be *sent*.

What do I do? Who am I now?
The answer eludes me.
Thy peace eludes me.
I stare through the window,
wondering what next.
There must be a *next!*
Is it too late to be *sent?*
Sent instead of spent?

I do not know where you are, O Lord.
I lean my forehead
against the cold cold glass,
longing for your light
in this dark dark night.

I still have a sense of calling,
but no one calls my name.

With New Sight Comes Insight

With new sight comes insight,
O Lord. Finally I see
in the dim moonlight
that I took the love
you offered me
and ran into the darkroom
of my dead soul,
swapping the gift of Life
for a photo in dull matte finish,
which I put on my resume.
Then they drove me out.

But you found me, O Lord!
I know that it is you
    speaking to me:

Calling me to a new
    definition of purpose
and a new vision of
    work as serving others—
as doing ministry,
not just making money.
Calling me to see
    your face in others

*One thing
I do know, that
though I was blind, now
I see."...*

*Jesus heard that they
had driven him out, and
when he found him, he
said, "Do you believe in
the Son of Man?" He
answered, "And who is
he, sir? Tell me, so that I
may believe in him."
Jesus said to him, "You
have seen him, and the
one speaking with you is
he." He said, "Lord, I
believe." And he wor-
shiped him.*

John 9:25, 35-38

and let your love shine through me.

Calling me to a new style
that balances being productive
with blessing others in the process.

Calling me to a new workplace
that is more than a marketplace,
that offers a sanctuary of meaning
which reaches beneath the surface
and beyond the self.

They nailed me to the cross.
But you speak to me of resurrection.
O Lord, I believe.

The pain of divorce touches us all. It
may come first through our parents' divorce,
as it did with me. Or through our own
divorce, or a sibling's, or that of a friend. Or
later, through the divorce of a grown child,
which may result in the additional pain of
separation from our grandchildren. Divorce
has touched my life in most of these ways,
and also through being a school counselor
and listening uncountable times to the pain
of children affected by divorce.

Divorce is a sunless wintery time and the
footing is slippery. There are not enough
quilts to warm the once-shared bed, and the
clock ticks loudly into the wee hours of the
night. To be healed requires a large dose of
courage to face the darkness and journey
through it.

"If only" is echoed in the silence of this
solitary journey: "If only" the *I do* had not
been said to the wrong person. And "What
if" follows in an icy whisper—"What if" life
in the future has no Christmas lights, no
seeds beneath the snow? When hands are

washed or a dinner fork lifted or a keyboard used, that bare fourth finger blares brokenness—broken promises, "broken" home, broken bits of smashed mementos. Perhaps a broken heart.

Connections taken for granted before become disconnected, like feeling as out of place with married friends as an eleventh pin in a bowling lane. Even talking to them can be a struggle, as though they suddenly need a foreign language. At work also some relationships change. And even at church. The former joy of worship on Sunday morning can become overshadowed by loneliness—that walk alone down the sanctuary aisle and no one saving a seat nor even offering to share a hymn book. And when worship is over, it seems that everyone else goes to eat in plurals, leaving a drive home alone to visible but noninteractive TV adults or invisible but interactive electronic chats. It is easy to wonder whether people would be less distant if one were widowed instead of divorced. They would send sympathy cards and show respect during a mourning period, and dignity is a given in that kind of loss.

In both "friendly" divorce and divorce due to betrayal, the pain of loss is present. When I think about my own parents' divorce, I still do not know even today whether it should have come sooner or not at all. But *shoulds*—"should have happened," "should not have happened"—are irrelevant in divorce. The reality is that it did happen. What matters in the aftermath is the healing of the heart. That healing is needed by both the parents and the children.

When evening came, his disciples went down to the sea, got into a boat, and started across the sea to Capernaum. It was now dark, and Jesus had not yet come to them. The sea became rough because a strong wind was blowing.

John 6:16-18

After All This Time

After all this time, O Lord,
my Ex snuffed out
 the unity candle.
Took one-and-one
and came up with three.
Leaving me
 with one-minus-one.
None.

I am being glib, O Lord.
I am always glib when I ache.
It keeps the pain at bay.

Over the years I saw life
in twos, duos, couples.
I lost *me* in *us*.
Went for double or nothing.
My Ex went for a triple play.
Sacrificed a spouse
to espouse the view
that new life could be found
with a new love.
Whatever happened, O Lord,
to renewed life

through renewed love?
We were two parts of a pair
like dice in a board game.
The two made a whole.
Being unpaired feels incomplete.
I am cast aside, half of nothing.

I allowed myself
to be used
misused
used up.
My Ex—now "X-Rated" in my review—
took me for "better"
and left me with "worse."
Scared and scarred
I lash out in return.
O Lord, will I still feel bitter
in thirty years?

Evening comes,
the hardest part of the day.
Alone I go down to the sea.
Alone I watch the sunset.
Alone I get into a boat and start across.

But it is dark now,
and I do not know how
to find the way.

I look for the moon,
and recall the full moons
with the one I loved.
Still love.
And hate.

I wish you were in this boat with me,
O Lord, but my spiritual life is buried
under the debris of divorce.
The sea is rough
and my sails are torn.
A strong wind is blowing.
Blowing me away.

Wounded and Numb

Wounded and numb, O Lord,
I stare at our wedding picture,
not feeling glib anymore.
My forehead seems branded
with a glow-in-the-dark letter *D*;
I know divorce is common
and happens all the time—
but not to *me*.

I have been asea
for months now
and rowed only
three or four miles
away from the shore,
with the storm
howling in my face
and the smell in the air
of dead dreams like dead fish,
and the bitter aftertaste
of being abandoned,
reaching out
for the hand
no longer there.

*When they
had rowed
about three or four miles,
they saw Jesus walking on
the sea and coming
near the boat, and they
were terrified.*

John 6:19

I do not know how to steer the ship
in the storm-tossed sea of single life
where I am expected to navigate
when my course is not charted
and I do not know the rules.

Sometimes now my dark side seems to reign,
exaggerating my weaknesses—
I overeat to fill the emptiness within,
fight greedily for things I do not even want,
and fantasize revenge.
I used to be confident
that I could get through things,
grow my way to the other side.
But I have never tried to grow alone.
Seeing no hope, no reason to care,
I surrender to despair.

As I scan the stormy sea
an apparition terrifies me.
O Lord, you are walking on the waves!
I rub the salt water from my eyes
but you are still there!

Are you coming near the boat?
Are you whispering my name?

Are you reaching for my hand?
Hiding from your Light, O Lord,
I lie down in the cold wet boat
and curl into fetal position,
letting the oars slip from my hands.

*But he [Jesus]
said to them,
"It is I; do not be afraid."
Then they wanted to take
him into the boat, and
immediately the boat
reached the land toward
which they were going.*

John 6:20-21

HUNKERING DOWN IN FEAR

Hunkering down in fear,
    O Lord,
I hear your words:
"Do not be afraid."
They pierce like a laser
through my layers
of self-deception.

You have watched me
two-step partnerless
through each day—
blame on the first beat,
shame on the second—
in the failed-marriage dance
of animosity and guilt.

Now you come
    into the boat with me
inviting me beyond shame,
    beyond fear.
I close my eyes
    and feel your palm
tenderly brush my forehead,
loving me as I am.

I see now that being "one"
is not at all being "none,"
and that awareness of incompleteness
begins the journey toward completeness.

Trusting you, I take your hand
and together we reach land—
the land within where the heart is healed.
O Lord, help me to become more than I am!
More than I was!

In life and light and love—
in God and Christ and Spirit—
I face toward the east window,
trusting resurrection once again,
watching for something unexpected
to be born anew in me.

WHEN IMPAIRMENT SNARES THE BODY

When I think of physical betrayal, the two most prominent people who come to mind are President Franklin Roosevelt and actor Christopher Reeve, one from a disease and the other from a horseback riding accident. Up close, my first friendship with a person with notable physical limitations began years ago. My friend, whose brilliant mind had little control over her frail body, was a member of the congregation my husband served. She wanted us to come to dinner, and we visited in the kitchen while she prepared the meal. I experienced her determination to do it all by herself and watched her hands go one way and the potatoes roll another way, over and over again. It left an indelible memory of the incredible patience, endurance, and extra time it takes to do tasks so simple for the rest of us who are "temporarily abled," to use a newer friend's phrase. For all of us who live long enough will experience betrayal by the body.

This newer friend, bright and blond, was going about her business as usual one day when the building she was in suddenly collapsed and she has been paralyzed ever since. She serves on a board with me, providing significant service from her wheelchair. Everyone who encounters her becomes aware that one whose body is physically *dis*abled can still be fully abled.

Many other friendships with people whose bodies are physically trapped have enriched my life. Two old friends, an attorney and a pastor, lost their agility when polio struck a few decades ago. Though both have been a bit slowed down over the years, one by a brace and the other by braces and crutches, neither perceives himself—nor is perceived by others—as "handicapped." They have made important contributions to their professions and continue to do so. Two other friends have diseases that deteriorate their muscles. They are less and less able to do what they once did. But both still chair task forces and live full lives. Another friend, an energetic CEO, recently went to work as usual, then suffered a severe stroke. He has not walked since—nor will he. Desire and determination, though helpful, cannot change the new physical reality of these situations.

My closest family member to experience sudden physical betrayal is my niece, with two young children and a brand new career. She went to bed one night and awoke later to a body changed beyond her recognition— a total stranger, paralyzed. Though she has made remarkable recovery, she has had to befriend that stranger to some degree, for it will never totally depart.

My own experience with physical vulnerability is so trivial it cannot be compared to any of the above. It merits mentioning only because of what it has taught me firsthand. I habitually bounded out of bed every morning of my life, eager to begin the day. During the process of writing this book, however, I awoke one morning and was shocked that I could not bound at all, but barely, slowly, painfully, sort of unkink one joint and muscle at a time. A "dysfunction" rather than a "disability," this minor and hopefully temporary impairment has shown me a different world. Now I know what it is like to unknot creakily instead of rise quickly, to have to concentrate on walking instead of taking it for granted, and to find simple things nearly impossible—like putting my leg over a bench to sit down at a long table. Now I know a new kind of vulnerability—making it upstairs only by pulling myself with my arms, and being too apprehensive to carry my grandson downstairs. Now I know a new kind of fear—wanting to ask a loved one to do something for me because of the difficulty of doing it myself, yet refraining from asking for fear it might become a habit. Not wanting friends to learn of my difficulty for fear I might become less independent, or begin to expect others to make exceptions for me, or use my difficulties as an excuse for negative behavior. All of these feelings and fears are new to me. This minor inconvenience—not at all a major impairment—has been a significant lesson in empathy.

Betrayal by the body is a source of fear, fear that brings on bad dreams—whether asleep or awake. The grief process is like being trapped in a room, looking for the secret knob to push that will open the concealed door to escape—and gradually coming to terms with the reality that there is not one. Vittorio Alfieri says something that especially fits the brave people who endure severe physical impairment: "Often the test of courage is not to die but to live."

This Debilitated Stranger

This debilitated stranger
cannot belong to me, O Lord—
not this body
    suddenly impaired!
Yesterday's served me well;
today's betrays me,
painful, limited,
unable to do my will.

Like a flash flood,
the change rolled in upon me.
Unexpected, irreversible,
for there is no
    Jerusalem for me,
no Sheep Gate, no porticoes,
    no pool,
and you do not happen by, Lord.

Unlike the man you saw,
I was agile in the past,
thriving on adventure, Lord:
Cross-country skiing
    in the moonlight
    at midnight.

*Now in
Jerusalem by
the Sheep Gate there is a
pool, called in Hebrew
Bethzatha, which has five
porticoes. In these lay
many invalids--blind,
lame, and paralyzed.
One man was there who
had been ill for thirty-
eight years. When Jesus
saw him lying there and
knew that he had been
there a long time, he said
to him, "Do you want to
be made well?"*

John 5:2-6

Hiking the Rockies,
    climbing Fourteeners,
    clinging to boulders,
    sliding through scree.
Mounting Bueno, the good Appaloosa,
    trotting up rugged slopes,
    picking the way down steep ravines,
    riding him like *The Man from Snowy River,*
    testing us both, as we became one.

Once I caught another's glance
and saw a hint of admiration in the eye
and maybe a wish to be more adventurous,
challenged physically, Lord, like me.

When people glance at me now,
the only hint in their eyes is relief
and gratitude that they are not
physically challenged, Lord, like me.

Even my friends look at me differently—
sort of round-about—
as though they should not look at me at all.
Do they see an invalid in the portico?
Invalid. In-valid. Not valid.
In others' eyes have I lost my validation
as a friend, a human being, a child of God?

O Lord, you asked the man
if he wanted to be healed.
Why do you not ask me!

The sick man answered him, "Sir, I have no one to put me into the pool when the water is stirred up; and while I am making my way, someone else steps down ahead of me." Jesus said to him, "Stand up, take your mat and walk." At once the man was made well, and he took up his mat and began to walk.

John 5:7-9

TRAPPED IN THIS CELL

Trapped in this cell, Lord,
with no parole,
I serve a life sentence—
the east window barred.

I live without living,
waiting for others
to wait upon me.
I do not want help, Lord!
I do not want pity!

I cry out to be restored
to the way I was before—
body, mind, and soul
in a synergetic whole.
You healed the man
by the pool, Lord,
but you do not heal me!

I try to do what you told him.
I *will* it. But will is not enough.
I cannot stand up,
take my mat and walk.

The waters suck me deep
into the dark womb of death, Lord.
Far beneath feeling, thinking, being.
    Down. Down. Down.
    Drown. Drown. Drown.
    I care not.
    Care not.
    Not.

Later Jesus found him in the temple and said to him, "See, you have been made well! Do not sin any more, so that nothing worse happens to you." The man went away and told the Jews that it was Jesus who had made him well. Therefore the Jews started persecuting Jesus, because he was doing such things on the sabbath. But Jesus answered them, "My Father is still working, and I also am working."

John 5:14-17

LIKE A STAINED-GLASS WINDOW

Like a stained-glass window
my life is shattered, O Lord;
the colorful shapes
that formed a pattern before
now jumble together,
broken pieces and whole ones
swirling in a kaleidoscope.

When you went
    to the temple, O Lord,
you found the man
    you had healed.
I, too, go to the temple
seeking you in the stillness.

I tell you my story though
    you already know it—
a story that begins,
    "Once upon a time"
way back in the cradle
when my soul was formed
    in you, O Lord.
But over the years

my soul was gradually impaired
by my masks
my vulnerabilities
my fear of risking new possibilities.
Now, with physical deformation
I sense my soul's reformation
and a deep transformation
into new wholeness.

I squint into the kaleidoscope
surprised by all the pieces
left untouched by this trauma, O Lord.
My life can form new patterns!
It is still brilliant in its colors!
It is still beautiful!
 For, O God, you are still working.
 O Jesus, you also are working.

Knowing there can be no change physically,
 I stand mentally,
 take up my mat emotionally,
 and begin to walk spiritually.
And in the silence of my heart, O Lord,
I hear your life-giving words speaking to me:
 See, you are being made well!

*D*arkness lingers
round me
but I rise to praise you, O God.
My chilled bones are cloaked
in the memory of your Word
lighting the way beyond pain
like a candle in the tomb,
inviting me to unwrap
your gift of hope.
I dance toward you
in the midnight mist,
breathing in your spirit and
feeling your heartbeat
in my own.
trusting your promise
of life after loss.

*R*emember
your word
to your servant, in which
you have made me hope.
This is my comfort in my
distress, that your
promise gives me life. . . .
At midnight I rise to
praise you.
Psalm 119:49-50, 62

FOUR
DANCING AT MIDNIGHT

Piet Mondrian's painting, *Red Tree*, is a writhing rendition of a single tree alone on the landscape, with reds hot against the dark blues of the night sky. The fire is the focus, scorching the tree. Orange flames lick around the trunk like burning oil atop midnight waters. The neck of the tree cowers backwards, twisting snakelike. The jagged branches rise in disarray, lifted in every direction like hair raised by lightning. Waves in deep shades of blue roll beyond the tree, waters present but too distant to save the tree from flames. Nowhere is there a hint of mauve to signal dawn and hope.

The ultimate losses—physical death, psychological death, and terminal illness—sear us like the red tree. Death can snatch a loved one, forcing us to survive the uttermost woundedness of our heart. Extreme psychological change can turn a loved one into a stranger, forcing us to endure the presence of a familiar physical body after the one we love has died relationally. Terminal illness can drain away our own life, forcing us to face our physical deterioration and make the journey toward death, not knowing how and feeling frightened. Or, instead, terminal illness can drain away the life of the beloved, forcing us to watch the mutiny of that body as we stand helplessly by.

As grievers of ultimate losses we climb
into Mondrian's flaming tree, isolating ourselves, the heat burning into our soul as our
world darkens into the blue-black midnight
of despair. We struggle to find meaning in
this loss, obsessed with the painful question
"Why?" But the flames leap without logic,
beyond understanding, devoid of meaning
and purpose. We experience constant con-
trast, paradox, ambiguity—for that is the
mystery of the cosmic dance. From the old
comes the new. From death comes life.
From chaos comes creation. From the cross
comes resurrection. The mystery behind rea-
sons makes up the symmetry of seasons.

During this season of sorrow, we walk on
an unknown path in a strange and lonely
land, strewing gray ashes along the way.
Though we have not moved, our world has
shifted. Like a child who dodged bombs in
Bosnia, we cannot make the journey without
being changed.

There comes a time in this season when
we realize that the lost one remains part of
our identity, permanently interwoven into
the very fabric of our being. Rooming in our

memory. Residing in our souls. Resting in the stillness of the Spirit. Though never again among us, never again apart from us through the mystery of creation.

The words of Isaiah speak to us: "the LORD will be your everlasting light, and your days of mourning shall be ended" (Isa. 60:20). And so, in the darkness and despair of midnight, we are invited to dance to the healing rhythm of grace.

WHEN A LOVED ONE DIES AND THE BODY LIVES

While a friend and I were walking along a lakeshore, we found a turtle shell in the sand. She bent and picked it up. The shell was hard, perfectly intact, but the life within had departed. That is how it seems to us when a loved one dies and the body lives. Instead of being empty, however, the original life in the shell has been exchanged for an imposter. We still feel responsible for the shell, but our hearts cry out with wonderings: *Why did the other have to leave? Why has this one entered who is so different?*

Because of my counseling background, I served for a while as a volunteer facilitator for a support group made up of those whose loved ones were in a United Methodist nursing home. The group dealt with the sadness caused by physical downturns of ones beloved, and their own guilt over not being able to care for them at home. They also struggled with the pressure of expectations they felt placed upon them. But the most pain-filled experiences in that group stemmed from encounters with loved ones whose personality and memory had altered; now they met a stranger who had taken over the familiar body of one beloved.

A dear friend experienced this kind of loss. Week after week she would see her "mother" and be beaten down by that alien residing in the body that had borne her. Sometimes my friend, with tears in her eyes, spoke of her own suffering. Once she shared her paraphrase of Joshua 1:9:

"Be strong and courageous";

I am weak and spineless; I cannot go on.

"do not be frightened"

I am terrified I will do this to my children someday.

"or dismayed,"

I spin in confusion and despair.

"for the LORD your God is with you wherever you go."

Then she added, "But God is with me when I am there. That is how I make it."

The grief process of mourning one who has died without dying is complex and confusing. In some ways, it is the most difficult loss to face, for it is a loss without loss, so to speak. It calls for a continually renewing strength that allows us to "mount up with wings like eagles, [to] run and not be weary, [to] walk and not faint" (Isa.40:31). When we visit a loved one and face one unknown, the complex dynamics include our own fear that we may "die" and leave our body behind, and thus we too may become a channel of hurt to those precious to us.

I think of an elderly friend who was a mentor for me in some ways. She was a woman of dignity and grace, interested in others, sensitive to their needs, a soft-spoken lady—in the very best sense of that term— married to a soft-spoken gentleman, equally kind. Now, a stranger has evicted that good woman, the kind of stranger whose behavior would have shocked her.

Community is a vital part of healing the heart in all kinds of loss. This is especially the case when a newcomer invades the body of one we treasure. How painful it is to stand in the presence of a person we love who is no longer the person we once knew! The caregiver needs care, too.

*After this
Jesus went to
the other side of the Sea of
Galilee, also called the
Sea of Tiberias. A large
crowd kept following him,
because they saw the
signs that he was doing
for the sick. Jesus went
up the mountain
and sat down there
with his disciples.*

John 6:1-3

ONLY THE SHELL

Only the shell
     is here before me.
I touch that hand,
     ever dependable
in gentle comfort
     and tedious toil.
Dear eyes glance at me,
     O Lord,
and the familiar mouth opens—
but a stranger speaks.

In anger and anguish, O Lord,
I watch this trespasser
who invaded the
     body of my loved one
like a promise taken away.
There is no joy, no tenderness
in this haunting presence
flaunting unyielding absence
mistreating family and friends
becoming a person our loved one
would not choose to become.

I smolder beneath the surface,
     O Lord,

feeling cheated and confused
longing to flee from this mocking thief,
trying to hide my hostility.

Help me, O Lord.
Mother Teresa encouraged us
to spread your fragrance everywhere we go
letting your life flood our souls
and shine on those around us.
But my faith dwindles
in the stench of this exchange.

It is as though one I cherished
became weary of the crowd
and like you, O Lord, crossed over the sea
and went up the mountain into retreat,
disappearing mentally far away from me.

When he looked up and saw a large crowd coming toward him, Jesus said to Philip, "Where are we to buy bread for these people to eat?" He said this to test him, for he himself knew what he was going to do. Philip answered him, "Six months' wages would not buy enough bread for each of them to get a little."

John 6:5-7

Old Memories Crowd This Space

Old memories
    crowd this space
where a stranger now resides,
and I long to be with the other
who sat at table with me
sharing the bread of love
and the wine of life, O Lord.

How can I connect
this awful change
    with the One of Awe?
This mysterious mutation
    with the One of Mystery?
This torture of my heart
    with the One of Tenderness?

Am I being tested, Lord?
This invader comes
    as one from the crowd,
unknown, extending
    an empty hand,
waiting to be served.
Am I expected to offer bread?

Do you not see that I have no bread to give?
Even half a year's wages would be too little
to buy solace to suffice,
for I cannot conquer my sense of loss,
    my grief,
    my despair.
O Lord, I cannot pass this test.

One of his
disciples, Andrew,
Simon Peter's brother,
said to him, "There is a
boy here who has five
barley loaves and two
fish. But what are they
among so many people?"
Jesus said, "Make the
people sit down." Now
there was a great deal of
grass in the place; so they
sat down, about five
thousand in all. Then
Jesus took the loaves, and
when he had given
thanks, he distributed
them to those who were
seated; so also the fish, as
much as they wanted.
When they were satisfied,
he told his disciples,
"Gather up the fragments
left over, so that nothing
may be lost."
John 6:8-12

ONE COMES BEARING BREAD

One comes bearing bread.
It is a small gift
inadequate in itself
but an amazing thing, O Lord,
a sharing amidst scarcity
a symbol of community.

Clutching a piece of that bread
I go to the park
and sit in the bountiful grass.

Bowed low by loss
I reflect
     meditate
     pray.

I see vividly that
     one gone away:
sharing the loaves and fishes—
no matter how meager,
     O Lord—
sharing with kinfolk
     and strangers alike
sharing in community.

The memory brushes my cheek
like a farewell kiss.

This is the Mystery!
Here in community
are compassion and care
and sharing in tender abundance.
Each of us has something to give—
a small piece of bread or a fish—
which put together, O Lord,
feeds us all.

I return to that body held captive,
now strengthened to care for the trespasser,
pondering absence in this presence
presence in this absence.
Could this one also have bread to give?

O Lord, could the stranger before me,
this shadow that remains,
somehow still be the one I love?
Not exchanged, but changed?
Mentally rearranged?

Help me, O Lord, to be grateful
for this last bit we share—

no longer the heart nor the mind,
no longer memories nor dreams—
but at least there is the same crooked grin,
the raised right eyebrow,
the habitual lift of the palm, fingers spread.
May this be enough
to sustain my starving heart.

I tear a piece from the loaf and offer bread.
Then dancing at midnight, O Lord,
I gather up the leftover fragments,
losing nothing.

WHEN TERMINAL ILLNESS STRIKES

As my husband and I left the worship service at Munger Place United Methodist Church in Dallas one morning, a woman greeted us and introduced herself. "My father was a pastor before he retired," she said. Then her smile disappeared along with the sparkle in her brown eyes, and she added softly, "He's terminal."

Terminal. The dreaded word. Doctors euphemize when speaking of that condition, carefully choosing words less direct, trying to be more tasteful. In the beginning, the ones affected by this diagnosis are also likely to approach it obliquely, unable to deal with it head on.

All of us, of course, are terminal. Ultimately, we share the same earthly destiny: death. We go along as though that is not so until something throws us into the face of that destiny, and suddenly we know that death—our own or a loved one's—is real, impending, coming sooner than we expected. The diagnosis starts a conscious countdown. Life expectancy leaps from the

abstract to the concrete: Days. Weeks.
Months. Maybe a year or two or three. Life
seems reduced to a series of ellipses with
the dots being deleted one at a time. A
death watch begins, a vigil kept day and
night, hearts staring toward the horizon as it
closes in.

This uninvited change changes us all. For
in terminal illness the person who is ill and
the ones who love that person must endure
not only loss itself but also the wrenching
prologue to loss. It is a journey we do not
know how to take and only learn as we
make our way through it, beginners again
each new day, seeking grace.

Once I visited a church in Tennessee,
where the cross had been removed from the
center of the chancel and placed off to the
side of the sanctuary, nearly hidden in the
shadows. The organ pipes protruded unob-
structed, front and center, offering the joyful
music of resurrection without the pain of
the cross. When affected directly or indirectly by terminal illness, we long to shove aside
this cross of pain so we can hear the music
of joy. Yet, our trust in God calls us toward

learning how to bear the cross front and center without being blind to the organ pipes in the background and deaf to the music of faith.

I do not yet know the perimeters that are around my own life. My experience with this frightening journey is through my courageous friends and family members who have walked it. Three faces I love come to mind: The first is a friend who has completed that journey, a journey I shared in *Wilderness Wanderings*. The second is a family member whose walk is now also completed. And the other is a member of our extended family who is making that journey now. The voice that speaks in the following prayers about this loss speaks on their behalf and on behalf of others who are in the midst of this prologue. Another voice is also offered, that of the loved one who faces the epilogue alone.

Then he came again to Cana in Galilee where he had changed the water into wine. Now there was a royal official whose son lay ill in Capernaum. When he heard that Jesus had come from Judea to Galilee, he went and begged him to come down and heal his son, for he was at the point of death.

John 4:46-47

ON THAT DAY AS EVERY DAY

On that day as every day—
as you know, O God,
but my soul cries
    out to you again—
the sun rose in Rio,
in Santa Fe, Sydney, and Seoul,
in Zagreb and Harare.
It shined on heights
    and depths
lush land and arid
a gift from you
to all your people.
    Except—I learned later,
    O God—except me!

On that day as every day—
as you know, O God,
but my soul
    cries out to you again—
the sea sang in the stillness
waves crested in
    cosmic harmony
a rooster greeted the morning

and a rock rose above the sea,
a rock scarred by dark graffiti.
    A portent—I learned later,
    O God—a portent intended for me!

On that day as no other day—
as you know, O God,
but my soul cries out to you again—
I sat with the doctor, whose eyes were grave,
and wound my way through his
    circle of words
until I grasped the dreaded translation:
    Terminal.

Dark clouds would shut out the sunrise,
a storm would stir the sea
the rooster would be silenced by mourning
and breakers would flood the shore
washing footprints forever from the sand.
    Footprints—I learned then,
    O God—footprints that belong to me.

    Terminal, *O Lord. The diagnosis of my
beloved shakes my bones. When we married, I did not fathom this—one of us
dying and one being left alone. I am not*

prepared for a dress rehearsal for death.

Death. *The word hisses at me. I back away. Distance myself. But how can I be close to my beloved from a distance? Can I go two directions at once, O Lord? I swallow tears, torn in half. I struggle for the courage to be a source of strength on this journey toward death, while a chunk of myself is dying, too.*

My gaze locks on the clock. One minute. Two. It no longer measures good moments on the journey together. It is the enemy, red hand spinning away the seconds toward separation. I want to jerk the clock off the wall. Stomp on it! Smash it to pieces!

O Lord, you returned to Cana where earlier you had changed water into wine. This time a stranger—a royal official, a Centurion, one from the enemy camp— begs you to heal his dying son. I too beg your help, O Lord. I who am not a stranger to you, not an enemy, but one of the family. A Christian. A Believer. I who adore you am in anguish. For death stalks my beloved.

O Lord, hear me! Do not ignore my plea! Do not let the sun of my life sink into the sea!

The Diagnosis Eclipsed the Sun

The diagnosis eclipsed the sun,
God. All is darkness.
The doctor's words rerun
deep and slow like a tape
whose battery is low.

I move in a daze, God,
through a mirrored maze,
the skull and crossbones
reflected all around me.

I strive to steady my
    trembling hands
that hold this new contract
with its undeserved terms,
this contract you have
    stuck in my face, God,
and my fingers refuse to sign.

Death hides behind
    the closet door.
"The creative role of
    death"—I read.

*Jesus said to him,
"Unless you see
signs and wonders
you will not believe."
The official said to him,
"Sir, come down before
my little boy dies." Jesus
said to him, "Go; your
son will live." The man
believed the word that
Jesus spoke to him and
started on his way.*
John 4:48-50

Head words! Not heart words!
Keep them in the seminars, the text books.
Do not bring them up close.
Keep your distance, Death!
Stay in the closet!

I am not ready to die!
Not ready to leave behind
everyone and everything I love—
my precious family and friends,
Christmas Eve communions,
wooded walks, table talk,
looking up at midnight stars
through the skylight above our bed.

O God, I am not ready for this final path
that leads to the end,
to the unknown.
I do not want to leave home!

I examine old memories
varied in patterns and textures
like scraps for a quilt.
Memories of children
of getting our first home
of heartaches and heartjoys,

of birthday celebrations with loved ones.
O God, will they still remember me
on my birthday?

Birthday. Deathday.
The quilt wraps around me,
the border reached, the edges bound.
O God, I want to
    add new pieces to my quilt!

My loved one sits beside me now
and I fake a smile, O God,
pretending nothing has changed
though nothing is the same.

I want to be fully awake,
*now*here,
missing not a moment,
losing not a wink of life.
Yet, I want also to be numb,
*no*where,
blank as an empty computer screen,
sparing myself the dread of death.

I long to be held, O God, yet I turn aside,
fearful that I will begin to weep.

How will my loved ones handle
my absent place at the table?
How I wish I could spare them this grief!

O God, why have you forsaken me?
I see myself framed in the window,
staring down like Dr. Zhivago
shivering amidst the icicles,
pen in hand beside a tiny candlelight,
writing my remaining days
wearing unraveling mittens.

*The diagnosis thunders in the back of
my mind, O Lord, in an endless lightning
storm. Without my beloved my home will
become cold stone, a musty museum of
glass-enclosed relics. How will I handle
that absent place at the table?*

*I can hardly bear to see my beloved
physically vulnerable, withering before my
eyes, sent out as a lone scout to battle
death's brigade. I do not want my beloved
to limp through this desert alone, O Lord,
but I do not know how to journey hand in
hand in this unknown land.*

*Each moment blinks its passing in the
neon light of finality. The last birthday.
The last Thanksgiving. The last Christmas.
All the things I left undone with my
beloved haunt me now, O Lord, as do all
the things I said I wish I had not said. I go
to sleep counting sins instead of sheep.*

*Why did we take so much for granted,
O Lord? Why did we miss all those spectacular sunsets? Life blurred from one day to
the next. Until now. The shadow of death
teaches me how to tell time. I touch that
dear hand and feel mine covered in return.*

*O Lord, the Centurion asked for your
presence, and you said his son would live.
I ask, too, Lord. I plead on my knees. But
no words come assuring me that my
beloved will not die. Do I who believed
beforehand go unheard? If I did not
believe, would you save my beloved, giving
me this sign so I would believe? Do you
grant an unbeliever more than a Believer?*

*From the abyss of anger and despair, I
shake my fist and cry out to you, O Lord.*

As he was going down, his slaves met him and told him that his child was alive. So he asked them the hour when he began to recover, and they said to him, "Yesterday at one in the afternoon the fever left him." The father realized that this was the hour when Jesus had said to him, "Your son will live." So he himself believed, along with his whole household.

John 4:51-52

ONE DAY CLOSER TO DEATH

One day closer to death,
   O Lord.
This has always been so,
   of course;
we are terminal from birth.
But now I *know*,
count down each day,
scratching a mark
on the prison wall of time.

I know about life, O Lord,
both living
   and pretending to live.
I know about the cross
   and resurrection,
but I know nothing about dying.
About death—yes.
But not dying.

The reality brings despair
but despair does not
   alter the reality.
Despair distorts
   my perceptions,

fades the colors around me,
fogs possibilities.
I plead for power against it.

O Lord, is it possible to live while I die?
Strengthen me to try.
Help me to *live* as each moment races
toward erasing all that I know.
Teach me each hour how to be alive in you
that you might be alive in me
for that, I know, is true Life.

O Lord, as I trust you with birth,
help me to trust you with death.
Birth and death—
polar ends of life
partners in the cosmic dance
proclaiming the natural rhythm of creation
the seasons of change
    that bring regeneration.

O Lord, help me
    to enter creatively into dying
to treasure the walk
on this final path
of life's journey,

a journey still savored
still sacred.

O Lord, I pray with folded hands
and feel my wedding ring.
Till death us do part.
Give me courage to unfold
the quilt of my life
and wrap it around my loved ones,
bringing tender closure to time together
and teaching them how to die.

O Lord, I believe you will not leave me
　　homeless
for I long to find a home in you
and become a partner in the Mystery,
dancing with the stars at midnight.

*Each morning brings me one day closer
to separation from my beloved, O Lord.
And from my own identity, for who I am—
me—is intertwined with we. I cannot—
will not—envision a future without this
one who is part of my very being.*

O Lord, despite my prayers, no one comes to meet me like they did the Centurion. No one greets me with the good news I long to hear. I, too, prayed yesterday at one o'clock, but there was no turn toward healing.

And there will be none! My beloved is going to die!

Though my soul still shouts "No!" my beloved's eyes now say a peaceful yes. I must not hand off my fears to this dear one, O Lord, who has come to trust the seasons.

But this season of death has come out of season. What we were putting together is incomplete. Death steals our future, O Lord. All that could have been is reduced to what was. Once more I clutch my beloved's hand, longing never to let go. Our wedding rings click, a presage of the emptiness to come.

Can I live while my beloved dies? I try to free myself from this pretense that nothing is different, this performance that belies my deepest self. O Lord, strengthen me. I do not want to rob my beloved and myself

*of authentic moments during this last slice
of time.*

*We pack a picnic and start down the
path of the final journey. Clearing our
tears, we see that the trail is lined with yellow columbines. We lift our cups, as
always, in remembrance of you, O Lord,
and in gratitude. Our communion awak-
ens precious dialogue.*

*From our wounded hearts we share our
stories. Stories that are current and those
that go back in time. Stories about ourselves and each other, stories that happened together and those that happened
apart, stories we have told many times and
those we have never shared before.*

*And in this sharing there is mystery, O
Lord. Our stories honor our souls—our
grieving, courageous souls. They connect
the ages, from generation to generation.
They transcend time and place, forming
patterns, which witness to the Story. They
combine into a pair of pieced quilts—one
complete, one incomplete—hanging side by
side, draped over the line of eternity and
blown by the Spirit.*

*Tonight, enfolding our hands and ten-
derly holding the heart of life, we watch the
spectacular desert sunset. We sit close—
touching, treasuring, savoring—making a
good memory that will warm my heart, O
Lord, when the freeze comes.*

*Streaks of color rest on the horizon, so
like the sunrise. Sunrise . . . sunset. One
coming . . . one going. Like birth and death.
The beginning and the ending. Both can
be beautiful. For both the coming and the
going are from you, O Lord.*

*My beloved smiles at me and speaks
with gentle strength: "When you look up
from your pillow through the skylight, I
will be there dancing with the stars at
midnight."*

*And healing, O Lord, healing begins
in me.*

When Death Separates

We saw public grief grasp the globe
when two women who graced the earth
died a few days apart, their funerals separat-
ed by a week. Both had titles followed by
first names. One was tall, the other small.
One was a fashion starter, the other barefoot
and wearing the same kind of sari from
decade to decade. One was young and died
being chased, her notable story interrupted
before the ending was known; the other was
elderly, peacefully ailing, her life-giving story
unchanged from chapter to chapter. One
had a flair for drama, capturing hearts en
masse through TV, the other modeled sim-
plicity—touching broken bodies one at a
time. One's son will be king, the other worshiped the Son she called King. One was a
princess, the other a nun. The deaths of
these two women, Princess Diana and
Mother Teresa, so different from one another,
brought the largest display of grief in the history of the world. People numbering in the
millions, in person and on TV, joined in
public grief.

Private grief is something else. My husband's mother, a woman I love dearly, died unexpectedly in her sleep. I remember walking down the lane at the farm, tears rolling down my cheeks, yet gratitude for her life welling up in my heart. As I walked that day and when I think of her now, the silent words of my prayer are always the same: *Thank you for the blessing.*

Death may come gently by giving a kiss in a peaceful sleep. Or mercifully after a long and painful illness. Or violently, leaping with extended claws. Or after relentless stalking, seducing a loved one toward suicide. In whatever way death comes, the life story of grievers is forever changed.

If there is a blessing in being the one left to mourn, perhaps it is the solace of sparing our loved one the agony of grief. Parker Palmer advises: "Do not avoid the places where the dead person once lived, the places where you knew life together with that person. Go there and be there; allow yourself to feel the anguish of utter loss." It is through our vulnerability that healing can begin.

In that loneliest place of void deep within us, we struggle to find meaning in the loss. We want to believe that everything that happens has meaning, but what is the meaning here? What is the pearl that can be discovered in the closed oyster of this painful journey? Palmer continues:

> Only as you do so [feel the anguish of utter loss] will you have a chance of being touched by the spirit of the dead one. Only so will you begin to understand that physical absence may yield a sense of presence more palpable than the body itself. Only so may you learn that life is never finally lost, only transformed.

It is as though our eyes, in time, gradually adjust to the dark and for an instant we glimpse the Mystery of being close to the heart of life.

The blaring struggle to find meaning in death can deafen us to faith's quiet call to accept the Mystery, and it is that call which brings peace. The stillness that comes to us as we release the struggle is not a silence of emptiness but of barefoot grace in the midnight dance with the Creator.

SMOKE RISES FROM THE CANDLE

Smoke rises from the candle
its flame snuffed out,
a flame that always glowed
in the window, O Lord,
welcoming me home.

My loved one
    is broken off from my life,
leaving me broken.
Anguish turns a crank,
stretching me on the rack.
Silence crackles around me
and my pain
    flares in the darkness.

I cry out to undo this tragedy,
    O Lord.
But no!
No rerun
no reprieve
no reordering of events
no replacement.
My loved one is gone.

*esus said
to them: "I am
the bread of life.
Whoever comes to me will
never be hungry, and
whoever believes in me
will never be thirsty."*
John 6:35

Without planning or preparation
    or premonition.
Without a good-bye.

Sometimes something happens
    that I want to share,
then suddenly I remember, O Lord,
that my loved one is not there.
Or I enter a favorite place
and for an instant
expect to see my lost one's face,
once again jolted by that empty space,
my senses on edge like newly cleaned teeth,
homeless without leaving home.

I want to binge to fill the void:
to work from dawn to dark
    till I fall asleep at my desk
to eat a whole chocolate cake
    and then another
to sojourn unmoving at the movies
to sit on the sofa in a TV-coma
to drink my senses dull.
I want to vent my rage.
To get revenge.
To go on a rampage.

Unable to bear the unbearable
I sever myself from myself
stand apart from my body, O Lord,
and watch me move in slow motion.
I hear my mouth speak words
    distanced from me
    as though framed
    in a cartoon balloon.
I see my head bend toward the rosebush,
    smelling the scent my loved one loved.
I observe my lips sipping mint tea,
    my eyes staring blankly across the table
    at that empty chair.
I notice my palms caressing the books
    alive with the touch of those dear hands.

The quicksand of grief sucks me under
without breath, without Spirit.
I, who ate of the bread, am hungry.
I, who was baptized, am thirsty.
Doubt consumes my faith.
Without faith, I have no hope.
Without hope, I walk in darkness.
I turn away from the Eucharist.
O Lord, I cannot drink this cup.

esus said, "I tell you most solemnly, everybody who believes has eternal life. I am the bread of life . . . I am the living bread which has come down from heaven.

Anyone who eats this bread will live for ever; and the bread that I shall give is my flesh, for the life of the world. . . . "

He taught this doctrine at Capernaum, in the synagogue. After hearing it, many of his followers said, "This is intolerable language. How could anyone accept it?" Jesus was aware that his follow-ers were complaining about it and said, "Does this upset you?"

John 6:47-48, 51, 59-61 (JB)

IN THE BLEAK JANUARY

In the bleak January
   of my soul
the breath of the Spirit
blows white in the air
and icicles weight down
the barren branch, O Lord.
My heart hides
   below the snow
and the stream of love
freezes hard as steel.

The Earth is a lesser place
as is my space upon it.

Remembering yesterdays
   when the sun rose,
I plod through
   month-long midnights
toward dreamless tomorrows,
somehow getting
   through each day,
O Lord, gray upon gray.

My strong will arms for battle

against despair, proving insufficient.
O Lord, how I miss those loving eyes
that gentle voice
that fragrance so familiar!
I gird my soul in knight's chain mail.

My dark side casts shadows,
and I want others to ache as I ache
I dwell on fantasies about placing blame—
as though to make another suffer
would make me suffer less.

I wall in, close out,
shrug off admonitions of others.
They fret and fuss, O Lord,
expecting me to be who I was.
And I am not. Cannot be.
I do not know who I am. Or will be.

I push the remote control
putting myself on auto-function,
even rendering an occasional hollow laugh,
startled by the sound.

Sometimes the retelling of the story
    reopens the wound,

and though well-meaning people
stand beside me, O Lord,
I hear them from the other side of a chasm,
their faces shrinking to doll size
their words firing at me across the distance,
     advising
     generalizing
     theorizing
     dogmatizing.
What I long for is a silent hug.

They do not know why
any more than I, O Lord.
There is no reason. No logic.
Life is not fair! Death is not just!
Sneering, fate writes on the blackboard
with squeaking chalk.

The doctrine taught at Capernaum
brings me no comfort.
It is the here and now
that concerns me, O Lord. Not eternity.
I wanted the one I love
to live forever in the flesh.
At least as long as I.
For it is the flesh that I know.

But the flesh is dead.
Yes! Like Capernaum,
     this is a difficult teaching!
Yes! I complain!
Yes! This upsets me.
Who can accept it?

My faith, once a thick spruce forest,
is reduced to scrubby cedars, O Lord,
scattered sparsely across
     the parched desert soil,
fighting stones for space.
A buzzard hovers.

> *It is the spirit*
> *that gives life; the*
> *flesh has nothing to offer.*
> *The words I have spoken*
> *to you are spirit and*
> *they are life.*
> John 6:63 (JB)

An Alien in the Land of Grief

An alien in the land of grief
even after all this time,
I awake seeking morning light
but mourning darkness,
    O Lord,
still presses in upon me.

Memories are all
    that I have left now,
so I wrap them tenderly
    in white tissue paper
and store them in the
    cedar chest of my heart,
cherished crumbs
    from our shared feast.

The morning prayer
    in my devotional guide
Spoke of following "through
    suffering to joy
and through death
    to resurrection."
Help me, to do that!

Help me to reach down in there, O Lord,
down into that deep space
down into my heart
into my soul.
Help me to reclaim my unlived-in life!

You said it is the spirit that gives life.
Renew my spirit, I pray.
Speak to me with those words
that are both spirit and life.

Yet even as I ask,
I know, O Lord, that you already have,
that all these months—
though I could not see it—
you have held a candle for me
that glowed in the window.

In stillness that arrives like a feather
I sense that my loved one is here with me
and always will be,
though now in a different way:
like cool shade on a hot summer day
or the last gold leaf on the aspen tree
or in the angel we bought
        our first Advent season

that I've placed on the tree
each Christmas Eve
or in the coming of the doves
building their nest on our porch
each spring.

A scripture comes to me, and I say it
over and over again in my mind:
"I can do all things through Christ
who strengthens me."

I fall on my knees, grateful, O Lord,
strengthened by your presence,
by this new way of being with my lost one,
by the hugs of my church family
surrounding me in love.
I drink fully of the cup, O Lord,
and rise from my knees
taking the first trembling step
to begin dancing at midnight.

I wait for you, O Lord,
staring into hopelessness
yet stirring toward hope
that Hope beyond
    shattered hopes,
which offers new life
and begins to heal my heart.
The emptiness of suffering
births the fullness of faith,
and the winds of the Spirit
lift me like a bird
soaring above
    the desert sands,
still while still moving.
I stand at the east window
waiting for sunrise,
trusting you, O Lord my God,
for it is you who will answer.

*It is for you,
O LORD, that I
wait; it is you, O LORD my
God, who will answer.*

Psalm 38:15

FIVE
WAITING FOR SUNRISE

In *The Rule of Benedict*,
Joan Chittister tells a story
from the ancients:

Once upon a time a disciple asked the elder, "Holy One, is there anything I can do to make myself Enlightened?"

And the Holy One answered, "As little as you can do to make the sun rise in the morning."

"Then of what use," the surprised disciple asked, "are the spiritual exercises you prescribe?"

"To make sure," the elder said, "that you are not asleep when the sun begins to rise."

We look through the east window so that we will not miss the sunrise when it comes.

Waiting for sunrise after deep loss is very difficult. In *The God Who Comes*, Carlo Carretto says, "Wait! Oh, the anguish of that 'wait,' the emptiness of that absence!" This time of waiting—this limbo, this neutral zone—feels like facing the past and walking backwards on a tightrope between what was and what will be. It is a time of dulled reasoning and heightened vulnerability. Whether this waiting period lasts a long or relatively short while, it is a time to be gentle with ourselves.

Carretto goes on to say, "But then, little

by little, I began to understand as never before, that [God] was present in the emptiness, in the waiting." This time of waiting is part of Thomas Kelly's "eternal now," but it is life in still-life form. Though our faith does not protect us from loss, it does assure us that God is present in the aftermath, in the waiting. Our faith gives us confidence that just as resurrection follows the cross, so new life follows loss.

Faithful waiting offers a calming dimension of trust that new life will unfold. As we wait for sunrise, loneliness shifts to time alone, and aloneness becomes solitude time, and solitude transforms into sacred time, God's time. It is a gift which can help us grow from embitterment toward empathy, from cynicism toward charity, from self-pity toward spiritual purpose. This time also helps us begin to find space for our loss, which will always be with us, but can be tucked tenderly in our heart instead of remaining our focus.

Faithful waiting also offers hope. In *Gratefulness, the Heart of Prayer,* Brother David Steindl-Rast speaks of biblical hope as "the stillness that waits for the flash of the

Lord's coming in any situation." *Any situation.* He says that "hope integrates. It makes whole." It is an "attitude of the heart, a basic bearing of the whole person." Hope is a "mark of spiritual wholeness," a "passion for the possible." Hope stands beside despair like an unopened present.

Faithful waiting, in time, offers a choice about our response to loss. Gerald Sittser and his family were returning from a happy vacation, and the world was wonderful. Suddenly a drunk driver smashed into them, killing family members from three generations—Sittser's small daughter, his wife, and his mother. In *A Grace Disguised,* Sittser writes:

> The experience of loss itself does not have to be the defining moment of our lives. Instead, the defining moment can be our response to the loss. It is not what happens to us that matters as much as what happens *in* us.

Sittser's response was tested not only by his tragic losses but also by the drunk driver's acquittal, for the driver's lawyer persuaded the jury that since he and his one passenger were both thrown from the car, the jurors could not be *sure* he was the one driving!

Faithful waiting offers courage in the face of our fear. Before Livingstone explored the Zambezi River and found what he called "Victoria Falls," they already had a name. The ancients had stood in awe, both of the falls and of the mist that rises like a white mushroom to meet the clouds in the sky. The Kololo people named the falls *Mosi-oa-Tunya*— "smoke that thunders." Fear is smoke that thunders.

Loss brings fear of the unknown. Fear of a future unlike the map we had drawn. Fear of darkness. Sittser writes:

> The quickest way for anyone to reach the sun and the light of day is not to run west, chasing after the setting sun, but to head east, plunging into the darkness until one comes to the sunrise.

We tend to *combat* fear, but better than fighting it is to welcome it to the table, bringing it out into the light. In the light of faith, fear can be reduced from thunder to a breath prayer.

Faithful waiting offers a way through the chaos that inevitably follows loss. Chaos *de*structs, but it also *con*structs. It is degenerative, but it is also regenerative. Chaos can be creative if we are not too reactive. The difference between the words *creation* and *reaction* is the placement of the letter *C*. "See." Where do we choose to place our "see"ing? What is our focus? Reactive or creative?

My husband and I visited refugee centers in Bosnia-Hercegovina in 1995. I heard the shelling and saw the bombed-out houses. I looked into the dead eyes of the old men, the sad eyes of the women, the frightened eyes of the children.

One woman who was in the Travnik refugee center, which housed five hundred people in twenty-seven rooms, stands out especially to me. Like the others, she had lived in a nice home in a lovely village and now had eighteen roommates who shared her space. Their sleeping pallets crowded the walls and beside each one was the refugee's possessions tied in a piece of cloth—the cherished mementos they had been able to carry when they fled for their lives, mementos reminding them of past comfort.

Like the others, she mourned her loved ones lost in the war, for the refugees knew that missing husbands, sons and fathers were doomed to the secret mass graves carved into the beautiful countryside, where the trees watched the massacres and wept.

Like the others, her cup overflowed with suffering and loss.

As I walked passed her crowded room, she was tending three young children. With the horrors of that war, she may or may not have been the children's "real" mother, but she was their mother now. In the midst of the chaos of scarcity in an overcrowded refugee center in a country ravaged by hostility, she was setting a small table and serving three little plates of food for the children, bringing abundant love and hospitality to one little corner of one little room.

When she saw me, she smiled. The children saw her smile, so they also looked up at me and smiled. I do not know that woman's

name. But her smile—that amazing smile—
is forever burned in my memory.

Unlike the others, whose response is so
understandable, her focus is clear. She is
involved in creation, not reaction. She com-
forts the children that God has given her in
the moment. She brings peace and perhaps
even joy to her tiny space. She witnesses to
life after loss.

When I think of that woman of courage, I
see the embodiment of Psalm 118:

> I was pushed hard, so that I was falling,
>> but the LORD helped me . . .
> This is the day the LORD has made;
>> let us rejoice and be glad in it.
>>> —Psalm. 118: 13, 24.

I do not know what direction the win-
dows of that little room face, but I do know
that in her mind she stands at the east window, and she will not be asleep when the
sun begins to rise.

As we bob along day to day like a tiny twig on the great Zambezi River, after finding our way out of the waterfall and through the strange land beyond it, we can be assured of two things. The river of life will lead to the waterfall of another loss. And there will be another sunrise.

You have turned my mourning into dancing; you have taken off my sackcloth and clothed me with joy, so that my soul may praise you and not be silent.

O Lord my God, I will give thanks to you forever.

Psalm 30:11-12

End Notes

Sources of quotations include :

PAGE 17. Parker J. Palmer, *The Active Life: Wisdom for Work, Creativity, and Caring* (San Francisco: HarperSanFrancisco, 1990), *pp. 40-41*.

PAGE 50. Thomas Merton, *The Way of Chuang Tzu* (New York: New Directions, 1995), *p. 42*.

PAGE 78. Vittorio Alfieri, cited in James E. Miller, *Winter Grief, Summer Grace: Returning to Life After a Loved One Dies* (Minneapolis: Augsburg, 1995), *p. 40*.

PAGE 120. Parker J. Palmer, *The Active Life: Wisdom for Work, Creativity, and Caring* (San Francisco: HarperSanFrancisco, 1990), *p. 151*.

PAGE 130. Phil. 4:13 (NKJV)

PAGE 131. *The Rule of Benedict: Insights for the Ages,* Joan Chittister (New York: Crossroad, 1997), *p. 32*.

PAGE 132:. Carlo Carretto, *The God Who Comes,* cited in Rueben P. Job and Norman Shawcuck, *A Guide to Prayer for Ministers and Other Servants* (Nashville, TN: The Upper Room, 1983), *p. 199, 200*.

PAGE 133. Brother David Steindl-Rast, *Gratefulness, the Heart of Prayer: An Approach to Life in Fullness* (Ramsey, NJ: Paulist Press, 1984), *pp. 138, 140, 143.*

PAGE 134. Gerald L. Sittser: A *Grace Disguised: How the Soul Grows Through Loss* (Grand Rapids, MI: Zondervan Publishing House, 1996), *p. 33.*

PAGE 134. Sittser, *p. 33.*